SEARCH FOR SYLVESTER

By
Anthony Tallarico

Copyright © 1992 Kidsbooks Inc. and Anthony Tallarico
7004 N. California Ave.
Chicago, IL 60645

ISBN: 0-8317-9319-8

This edition published in 1992 by SMITHMARK Publishers Inc.,
112 Madison Avenue, New York, NY 10016

All rights reserved including the right
of reproduction in whole or in part in any form.

SMITHMARK books are available for bulk purchase for sales promotion and premium use.
For details write or telephone the Manager of Special Sales, SMITHMARK Publishers Inc.,
112 Madison Avenue, New York, NY 10016. (212) 532-6600.
Manufactured in the United States of America

Sylvester has run out of bamboo shoots to eat, but the mall should be the perfect place to buy some more.

SEARCH FOR SYLVESTER AT THIS MAD MALL AND...

- ☐ Banana peel
- ☐ Bird
- ☐ Birdhouse
- ☐ Bow and arrow
- ☐ Bowling ball
- ☐ Bride
- ☐ Cactus
- ☐ Convict
- ☐ Crown
- ☐ Dog
- ☐ Dracula
- ☐ Drum
- ☐ Feathers (2)
- ☐ Fish (2)
- ☐ Football
- ☐ Heart
- ☐ Ice-cream cone
- ☐ Jack-in-the-box
- ☐ Jack-o'-lantern
- ☐ Lion
- ☐ Moose
- ☐ Pig
- ☐ Rabbit
- ☐ Sailboat
- ☐ Santa Claus
- ☐ Star
- ☐ Surfboard
- ☐ Toy panda
- ☐ Trumpet
- ☐ Tuba
- ☐ Turtle
- ☐ Umbrella

ZAPPED! ELECTRONICS
VIDEO GAMES ZONE
I FEEL MUCH BETTER WITH A NEW BATTERY!!
PING!
PONG!
BINK!
DO NOT READ THIS!
ZIPP!
THIIIIG!
I MUST HAVE TAKEN A WRONG TURN!
QUIET!
WHERE DID I PARK MY SPACECRAFT?
I LOST MY MARCHING BAND!
WHO PUT SOAPY WATER IN MY TUBA?
SHOP 'TIL YOU DROP!
WHERE'S THE SURF?
I'M GOING UP!
I ESCAPED!
PIZZA
NO YOU DIDN'T!
I FEEL LIKE A KING TODAY!
STUFFED ZOO
NOT WELCOME KEEP OUT!
WHICH WAY?
WHERE IS THE YELLOW BRICK ROAD?
INFORMATION
IT WORKS.
BLATT!
I DON'T ANSWER HOMEWORK EXAMS!!

Sylvester had no luck at the mall, so he figured he'd try the park next. Boy, was he getting hungry!

SEARCH FOR SYLVESTER IN THIS FUN-FILLED PLAYGROUND AND...

- ☐ Artist's model
- ☐ Balloons (3)
- ☐ Baseball cap
- ☐ Birds (4)
- ☐ Cactus
- ☐ Cat
- ☐ Chef's hat
- ☐ Clipboard
- ☐ Crown
- ☐ Drum
- ☐ Ducklings (4)
- ☐ Fish
- ☐ Fisherman
- ☐ Fork
- ☐ Genie
- ☐ Graduate
- ☐ Hammer
- ☐ Heart
- ☐ Mailbox
- ☐ Mouse
- ☐ Paintbrush
- ☐ Pencils (2)
- ☐ Postal carrier
- ☐ Rabbit
- ☐ Roller skates
- ☐ Saddle
- ☐ Sailboats (2)
- ☐ Saws (2)
- ☐ Scooter
- ☐ Squirrel
- ☐ Sunglasses
- ☐ Top hat
- ☐ Trash basket
- ☐ Umbrella

What's for rent?
What's the price of a pickle?

I'M CHARLES OF THE CHIMPS!
THIS IS YOUR PARK ... KEEP IT CLEAN!
I'M ALL OUT OF BAMBOO SHOOTS.
EATS
YOU ARE HERE ✕
HOW ABOUT CARROTS?
LET'S GO, DUCKLINGS.
I'M GETTING WET.
HAVE YOU SEEN CAPTAIN AHAB ?
NO ICE SKATING TODAY!
WAIT FOR ME!
TELEPHONE
DON'T YOU DARE STRIKE ME!
I'M JUST A GUTTER BALL!

There were no bamboo shoots in the park, so Sylvester stopped off at a place where they serve almost anything!
SEARCH FOR SYLVESTER AT FAST FOOD HEAVEN AND...
☐ Arrows (2)
☐ Bone
☐ Cactus
☐ Cane
☐ Chef
☐ Crocodile
☐ Dogs (2)
☐ Drummer
☐ Earmuffs
☐ Elephants (2)
☐ Flying bat
☐ Flying carpet
☐ Flying saucer
☐ Fork
☐ Gas mask
☐ Ghosts (2)
☐ Green balloons (3)
☐ Igloo
☐ Kangaroo
☐ King
☐ Knight
☐ Lion
☐ Net
☐ Octopus
☐ Owl
☐ Pig
☐ Queen
☐ Santa Claus
☐ Skunk
☐ Squirrel
☐ Top hat
☐ Tuba
☐ Turtle
☐ Viking
Who hopes that the fish is fresh?
THIS IS JUST LIKE SCHOOL!
IS THE FISH FRESH?
TOOT-TOOT!
TOOT-TOOT-TOOT!
ME, TOO!
I'M STAYING HERE.
I ATE!
I'M EIGHT.
WHO?
IS THAT A PIGSKIN YOU'RE HOLDING?
THIS IS THE PLACE!
DO THEY SERVE BONES?
I'M LATE FOR LUNCH.
HO-HO! OH-NO!!
I USUALLY EAT HERE AT NIGHT.
I WANT GHOST TOASTIES.
DOWN WITH TURTLE SOUP!
HEY, HAY!
MD
WHEN DO THEY CLOSE?
WHEN THE BOARD OF HEALTH ARRIVES!
HOW DO I EAT WEARING THIS?

FAST FOOD HEAVEN.... FAST FOOD HEAVEN
SOUR PICKLES
DANGER BEANS
PUDDING PIZZA
PEPPERONI!
BUBBLEGUM SOUP
BANG!
IT'S STICKY!
SOUR SAUERKRAUT
HELP! I'M DROWNING!
EVERYTHING HAMBURGERS
GROSS.
HOT DOGS
IT'S HOT!
IT'S A DOG!
COLD CATS
MEOW, BRRR!
MUD STEW
IT'S MUDDY!
MYSTERY MEALS
I DON'T KNOW!
?
SPITGHETTI
IT TASTES BETTER THIS WAY!!
BLAZING CHILI
A LITTLE TOO HOT!
SUSHI
I LIKE MINE WELL DONE!!
FAST FOOD HEAVEN
BAMBOO
SOLD OUT
JUNK FOOD
LET ME AT IT!!
WE HAVE IT ALL!!
THAT WAS GREAT.
FROG'S LEGS
LOOKS GOOD.
I'M ON THE MENU.
MONSTER MEALS
DID YOU PAY YOUR BILL?
I HOPE THEY DON'T SERVE KANGAROO STEW HERE!!
I'M HUNGRY!
I ATE EVERYTHING!
DO YOU NEED HELP WITH THAT?

"The zoo should have bamboo shoots," thought Sylvester after he failed to find any at FAST FOOD HEAVEN. So off he went.

SEARCH FOR SYLVESTER AT THE ZANY ZOO AND...

- ☐ Artist
- ☐ Balloon
- ☐ Basket
- ☐ Bat and ball
- ☐ Bear
- ☐ Birds (2)
- ☐ Brooms (2)
- ☐ Buzzard
- ☐ Candy cane
- ☐ Cook
- ☐ Crown
- ☐ Dracula
- ☐ Duck
- ☐ Flamingo
- ☐ Graduate
- ☐ Ice-cream cones (2)
- ☐ Key
- ☐ Monkey
- ☐ Mouse
- ☐ Painted egg
- ☐ Pencils (2)
- ☐ Penguin
- ☐ "Polly"
- ☐ Rabbit
- ☐ Rooster
- ☐ Sailboat
- ☐ Seahorse
- ☐ Spoon
- ☐ Toucan
- ☐ Toy ship

Who doesn't know?
Who is going back to Transylvania?

I'M GOING BACK TO TRANSYLVANIA.
MORE GIFTS SHOP
I LOST THE RECIPE FOR BAMBOO SHOOTS!
I'LL INFORM HIM!
I DIDN'T DO IT!!
I DON'T HAVE BAMBOO IN MY TANK!
IT'S A GREAT VIEW FROM UP HERE!
FOR RENT
I DON'T HAVE ANY, SYLVESTER!
I'M A BUZZARD. I EAT EVERYTHING.
I'M LOOKING FOR SOME PEANUTS, MYSELF.
I'D RATHER HAVE A STEAK!
A TOUCAN WON'T EAT THAT.
I'VE NEVER HEARD OF THAT!
I'M THIRSTY.
DO FEED ME!
I'D RATHER HOLD AN ICE-CREAM CONE.
HOLD STILL.
OKAY! I'LL HOLD STILL!
I'M JOE STILL!

Sylvester had no luck finding bamboo shoots at the zoo, but his next stop is the ABCD school lunchroom. He's sure to find bamboo shoots there.

SEARCH FOR SYLVESTER IN THIS ALPHABETICAL SCHOOL AND...

- ☐ A
- ☐ B
- ☐ C
- ☐ D
- ☐ E
- ☐ F
- ☐ G
- ☐ H
- ☐ I
- ☐ J
- ☐ K
- ☐ L
- ☐ M
- ☐ N
- ☐ O
- ☐ P
- ☐ Q
- ☐ R
- ☐ S
- ☐ T
- ☐ U
- ☐ V
- ☐ W
- ☐ X
- ☐ Y
- ☐ Z
- ☐ Baseball cap
- ☐ Eyeglasses
- ☐ Spoon

What kind of prehistoric animal is it?

I HAD LUNCH.
YOU'RE LUCKY.
IS THIS THE GYM?
EAT WITH US!
COME ON OVER.
THERE'S A PANDA IN THIS ROOM!
I THINK IT'S TIME FOR RECESS!
I'M NOT ON THE TEAM. I JUST CAN'T GET IT OFF!!
I'M GOING TO THE MALL AFTER SCHOOL.
WHAT'S ON THE MENU?
I DON'T KNOW!
PEANUT BUTTER AND BLUBBER.
THAT SOUNDS GOOD!
GOOD ENOUGH TO LEAVE THIS LINE!
WHAT SMELLS GOOD?
MY SNEAKERS.
SAVE ME A SPOT!
BAMBOO SHOOTS?
I'M GLAD I'M ON A DIET!
SOMEONE ASKED ME FOR BAMBOO SHOOTS.
I'M IN THE SCHOOL PLAY.
ARE YOU WEARING A MASK?
YOU MISSED
THAT'S A GREAT IDEA!!
I'LL MAKE IT TOMORROW.
GET ME OUT OF HERE!

They were not serving bamboo shoots for lunch, but as Sylvester was leaving he heard cheering coming from the gym. "Maybe, they're selling bamboo shoots in there," he thought.

SEARCH FOR SYLVESTER AT THE BASKETBALL GAME AND...

- ☐ Baskets (2)
- ☐ Bird
- ☐ Bone
- ☐ Book
- ☐ Bunny
- ☐ Cleats
- ☐ Clown
- ☐ Dogs (2)
- ☐ Doughnut
- ☐ Elephant
- ☐ Envelopes (2)
- ☐ Fish
- ☐ Flower
- ☐ Football
- ☐ Frog
- ☐ Glove
- ☐ Horn
- ☐ Ice skate
- ☐ Ice-cream cone
- ☐ Juggler
- ☐ Mouse
- ☐ Necktie
- ☐ Popcorn
- ☐ Roller skates
- ☐ Sailor's cap
- ☐ Saw
- ☐ Slice of pizza
- ☐ Snake
- ☐ Stars (3)
- ☐ Toy arrow
- ☐ Whistle

Who wants to play, too?
Who is winning?

GO... GO... GO TEAM!!
I WANT TO PLAY, TOO!
BASKETBALL PLAYERS LIKE TO DUNK DOUGHNUTS!
THEY ALWAYS CARRY HANKIES BECAUSE THEY DRIBBLE.
I'M HERE TO MAKE SURE NO ONE STEALS THE BALL.
I LIKE TO MAKE BASKETS, TOO!
GO FOR IT!
THANKS.
THROW IT TO ME.
WHO HAS THE BALL?
NOT ME!
I CAN JUMP FURTHER THAN YOU.
I'M IN THE WRONG PLACE.
DON'T TICKLE ME!
WHAT'S GOING ON HERE?
I'M GOING TO SHOOT!
TOSS IT HERE!
HOW MANY SIDES DOES A BASKETBALL HAVE?
I NEVER GET THE BALL.
TWO! THE INSIDE AND THE OUTSIDE!
WHICH WAY?
NO BALL PLAYING

Not a single bamboo shoot was sold at the game. Sylvester was starving. He passed an old haunted house where someone was cooking. Could they be making bamboo shoots?

SEARCH FOR SYLVESTER AT THIS SPOOKY MANSION AND...

- ☐ Apple
- ☐ Arrows (2)
- ☐ Banana
- ☐ Bone
- ☐ Button
- ☐ Can
- ☐ Cook
- ☐ Cup
- ☐ Cupcake
- ☐ Fire hydrant
- ☐ Flashlight
- ☐ Flowerpot
- ☐ Heart
- ☐ Ice-cream soda
- ☐ Jack-o'-lantern
- ☐ Keyboard
- ☐ Kite
- ☐ Mask
- ☐ Medal
- ☐ Old shoe
- ☐ Pencil
- ☐ Pie
- ☐ Pot
- ☐ Pumpkin
- ☐ Rat
- ☐ Ring
- ☐ Skateboard
- ☐ Skulls (2)
- ☐ Sled
- ☐ Street light
- ☐ Sword
- ☐ Swordfish
- ☐ Trash can
- ☐ Turtle
- ☐ Umbrella

COME ON IN!
YOO-HOO! SYLVESTER!
I'LL GET HIM FOR YOU!!
LET ME GET HIM!
NOT WELCOME
SYLVESTER TASTES BETTER THAN BAMBOO!
FOR RENT

Sylvester didn't enter the haunted house, and now he was really, really hungry. "Maybe Detective Donald can help me detect bamboo shoots," thought Sylvester.

SEARCH FOR SYLVESTER AT DETECTIVE DONALD'S DIGS AND...

- ☐ Apple core
- ☐ Beard and glasses disguise
- ☐ Blackboard
- ☐ Bomb
- ☐ Boot
- ☐ Broken legs (2)
- ☐ Broken pencils (3)
- ☐ Buckets (2)
- ☐ Candles (3)
- ☐ Cupcake
- ☐ Dart
- ☐ Deflated balloon
- ☐ Dumbbell
- ☐ Eraser
- ☐ Feather
- ☐ Fish
- ☐ Fly swatter
- ☐ Footprints
- ☐ Graduation cap
- ☐ Hamburger
- ☐ Hockey stick
- ☐ Hole in a shoe
- ☐ Hooks (3)
- ☐ Hourglass
- ☐ Ink bottle
- ☐ Mirror
- ☐ Mouse
- ☐ Owl
- ☐ Paintbrush
- ☐ Record
- ☐ Ring
- ☐ Roller skate
- ☐ Slice of pizza
- ☐ Stars (3)

SQUEAK!
SQUEAK!
SQUEAK!
SHERLOCK HOLMES FAN CLUB
NO BAMBOO HERE!
DONALD
DIPLOMA
I DETECT A CLIENT.
MUD MAGAZINE
SPORTS ILL-STATED
SOAP BOX
I WANT TO DETECT DONALD.
A GIFT ESPECIALLY FOR DETECTIVE DONALD

Detective Donald advised Sylvester to look under the big top for bamboo shoots.

SEARCH FOR SYLVESTER AT THIS SILLY CIRCUS AND...

- ☐ Baker
- ☐ Banana
- ☐ Bat
- ☐ Bearded man
- ☐ Binoculars
- ☐ Candy cane
- ☐ Carrot
- ☐ Clothespins (3)
- ☐ Cup
- ☐ Dog
- ☐ Elephants (2)
- ☐ Feather
- ☐ Fire hydrant
- ☐ Giraffe
- ☐ Hot dog
- ☐ Humpty Dumpty
- ☐ Ice skates
- ☐ Ice-cream cone
- ☐ Kangaroo
- ☐ Lamp
- ☐ Mice (2)
- ☐ Mother Goose
- ☐ Paint bucket
- ☐ Paper bag
- ☐ Periscope
- ☐ Pig
- ☐ Pillow
- ☐ Rabbit
- ☐ Seals (2)
- ☐ Skunk
- ☐ Slice of watermelon
- ☐ Stars (5)
- ☐ Top hat
- ☐ Turtle
- ☐ Umbrella
- ☐ Unicorn
- ☐ Watering can
- ☐ Wizard

Who lost his costume?

WHERE'S THE MUSTARD?
KEEP OFF!
I WANT TO GET DOWN.
I QUIT!
I WANT TO GET DOWN, TOO!
DONALD WAS WRONG! THERE ARE NO BAMBOO SHOOTS HERE.
OU DO THAT
ERY WELL!
SNAP!
SNAP!
SNAP!
ULP!
CAN I JOIN THE CIRCUS?
I'M FROM THE BIG APPLE!
SNAP!
ME, TOO!
THIS IS THE BEST SEAT IN THE TENT!
BOOM!
DRIP-DRIP-DRIP!
DO DROP IN!
THIS IS A STRANGE PLACE!
WE'LL CATCH YOU!
LET'S GO BACK TO OUR PLANET!
I DON'T HAVE A LICENSE TO FLY!
YOU LOOK GOOD.
I'M THIRSTY.
MY
AVORITE
OLOR.
DON'T FORGET TO WRITE!
THAT'S A SILLY HAT!
I LOST MY COSTUME.
THIS IS MY DAY OFF!
OINK.
HI!

Sylvester had no luck at the circus, but on his way home he spotted a hot air balloon about to take off. "From up there I'll be able to find bamboo shoots," thought Sylvester.

SEARCH FOR SYLVESTER AS HE SOARS THROUGH THE SKY AND...

- ☐ Alien spaceship
- ☐ Ape
- ☐ Apple
- ☐ Arrows (2)
- ☐ Books (2)
- ☐ Bowling balls (2)
- ☐ Broom
- ☐ Candy canes (2)
- ☐ Chef
- ☐ Clowns (2)
- ☐ Coffeepot
- ☐ Cup
- ☐ Ducks (2)
- ☐ Firecracker
- ☐ Fish (2)
- ☐ Fishing pole
- ☐ Flowerpot
- ☐ Footballs (2)
- ☐ Hearts (2)
- ☐ Horns (2)
- ☐ Hose
- ☐ Hot dog
- ☐ Light bulb
- ☐ Lips
- ☐ Magnifying glasses (2)
- ☐ Painted eggs (2)
- ☐ Pencil
- ☐ Pillow
- ☐ Slices of watermelon (2)
- ☐ Telescopes (2)
- ☐ Tires (2)
- ☐ Turtles (2)

Who is the witch talking to?

THIS IS BETTER THAN CLIMBING THE EMPIRE STATE BUILDING!
COME OVER HERE!
I CAN'T COOK BAMBOO SHOOTS!
I'M A STAR! R-U?
THE SKY IS CROWDED.
I'M A MOVIE STAR.
I DON'T SEE ANY BAMBOO SHOOTS!
IS IT RAINING?
I'M A ROCK STAR!
WE'VE BEEN SHOT DOWN!
IS THAT YOU, JUNIOR?
KEEP OFF THE GRASS
HOT AIR BALLOON MEET TODAY
OOPS!
NICE SHOT!

From way up above Sylvester saw his old neighborhood. "That's it!" thought Sylvester. "I should have known to go back home to mom."

SEARCH FOR SYLVESTER IN BAMBOO TOWN AND...

- ☐ Apple
- ☐ Artist
- ☐ Backpack
- ☐ Birds (3)
- ☐ Bone
- ☐ Bucket
- ☐ Cactus
- ☐ Cash register
- ☐ Cat
- ☐ Crowns (2)
- ☐ Dogs (2)
- ☐ Elephant
- ☐ Feather
- ☐ Fish (3)
- ☐ Hammer
- ☐ Hoe
- ☐ Key
- ☐ Kiddie pool
- ☐ Mailbox
- ☐ Mushroom
- ☐ Photographer
- ☐ Pie
- ☐ Pitcher
- ☐ Pitchfork
- ☐ Pumpkin
- ☐ Scarecrow
- ☐ Scissors
- ☐ Scooter
- ☐ Screwdriver
- ☐ Sword
- ☐ Tricycle
- ☐ Turtles (2)
- ☐ Umbrella

What is the name of the street?
Who is "Captain Bamboo"?

GIANT BAMBOO STALKS OFTEN GROW TO A HEIGHT OF 120 FEET!
BIG GUY!
BIG SHOW OFF!
HI, SYLVESTER!
I LIKE TO BOO BAMBOO!
DO NOT PICK THE BAMBOO!
BAMBOO IS A GIANT GRASS!
I'M LOST!
SYLVESTER'S HOME
UP WITH BAMBOO SHOOTS!
BAMBOO
THERE ARE ABOUT 500 DIFFERENT TYPES OF BAMBOO!
A BAMBOO CAN GROW AS TALL AS 36 INCHES IN 24 HOURS.
I LIVE IN A BAMBOO BIRDCAGE.
HE'S COMING HOME.
THIS IS THE BEST PLACE TO FIND BAMBOO SHOOTS.
CAPTAIN BAMBOO IS MY SUPER HERO!
SYLVESTER, I MADE YOU A BAMBOO SHOOTS PIE!!
GET OFF THE GRASS.
CAPTAIN BAMBOO
I'M MAKING A BAMBOO BASKET.
I LIKE MY BAMBOO FISHING POLE.
61
I'M GOING IN FOR A DIP!
ME, TOO!
BAMBOO SHOOTS PIZZA EXPRESS
I'LL BE RIGHT BACK.
OCTOPUS CROSSING
I'M GOING TO WORK.
BAMBOO SHOOTS PIZZA EXPRESS
HURRY! WE HAVE A LOT MORE TO DELIVER!
BAMBOO SHOOTS PIZZA EXPRESS!
BAMBOO SHOOTS PIZZA EXPRESS
OFF TO WORK WE GO!
DID WE ORDER PIZZA?
NO, BUT WE SHOULD HAVE.
I DON'T WORK!

Syvlester ate all the bamboo shoots he wanted yesterday, but today he woke up hungry again!

SEARCH FOR SYLVESTER AND...

- ☐ Candy cane
- ☐ Envelope
- ☐ Flamingo
- ☐ Flying bat
- ☐ Hearts (2)
- ☐ Horseshoe
- ☐ Light bulb
- ☐ Mushroom
- ☐ Musical notes (2)
- ☐ Painted eggs (2)
- ☐ Picture
- ☐ Pitcher
- ☐ Raccoon
- ☐ Stars (2)

SEARCH FOR SYLVESTER